Hands & Feet

Hands & Feet

100 pampering tricks

Carol Morley & Liz Wilde

MQP
MQ Publications Ltd

introduction

Look your best from the tips of your fingers to the ends of your toes! Pamper your extremities and treat yourself to a little indulgence. Here are 100 professional tips sure to get your nails into tip-top condition, including how to do a full manicure and pedicure, the secrets of massage, how to cheat with false nails, how to have baby-soft feet, and even a home guide to reflexology. No more excuses for bitten nails and ragged cuticles; this little book will have your hands and feet looking better than you thought possible!

NAIL BRUSH

SOAP

contents

chapter 1

Manicure basics

1 **Nail salons have never been so big, and investing in a professional manicure means you're more likely to carry on the good work at home.** Treat yourself once a month and watch your manicurist carefully. You can pick up tricks to use at home.

2 **Make a professional manicure last longer by taking in your own polish.** That way you can touch up at home.

3 **A professional polish job is done with three strokes:** One straight down the middle from base to tip, and then one on both sides, avoiding the edges to elongate the nail. Keep a cotton ball soaked in remover at hand to correct any mistakes. But don't get too attached to your polish—most manicurists believe in the six-days-painted, one-day-off rule to give your nails a chance to breathe.

4 **Instead of soaking your nails in warm soapy water,** add a few drops of bath or baby oil to hot water for softer hands and cuticles. Then gently push cuticles back with a rubber-tipped cuticle stick or an orange stick wrapped in cotton that has been soaked in cuticle remover (avoid any metal manicure tools). Never cut cuticles since this removes the nail's protective layer, letting bacteria get underneath. And don't try to push cuticles back when your nails are dry. Injuries happen that way, and a blow to the nail bed means a ridge that can last for months (nails grow less than $1/16$ inch a week, so it can take up to four months for a nail to renew itself).

5 **There's no need to scrub when removing old polish.** Use an acetone-free remover, which won't dry out your nails (look for bottles labeled "conditioning" and "gentle"), and press a soaked cotton cosmetic pad onto each nail for a few seconds before wiping. Even the darkest color will come off in one stroke.

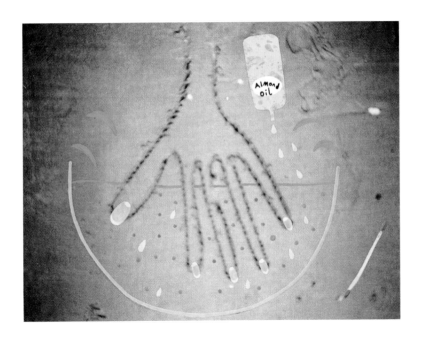

6 Manicure law: Never file your nails backwards and forwards. To avoid splitting, it is important to work in one direction only with the wide end of an emery board. Use the coarser side for shortening your nails, and use the finer side for the final finishing and shaping. Treat yourself and buy the slightly more expensive padded emery boards, which are much kinder to your nails than the cheaper ones, which resemble strips of sandpaper. One last thing: Don't go too deeply down at the corners when filing your nails as this makes them weak and prone to breaking.

7 Strong, healthy nails need a diet containing protein, vitamins, and minerals, including zinc and iodine. Brittle nails may mean a vitamin A deficiency, and hangnails could be hankering for folic acid (found in liver and green vegetables). And despite the calcium myth, white spots are actually a sign that you need more zinc. Experts are divided on whether eating gelatin has any effect on weak nails. Because gelatin is made from the bones of animals, it makes sense that the protein in bone and bone marrow could help the health and strength of your own nails, teeth, and bones.

file

8 **No time to paint on polish?** Then buff your nails to a natural shine. Like filing, you should go only in one direction. Work from base to tip with rapid movements, but stop if you feel the burn. P.S. In a recent poll, women who wore nail polish were considered less trustworthy than women who go natural. You have been warned!

9 **Healthy nails need good blood circulation in the nail bed** to ensure delivery of oxygen and essential nutrients. Get yours going with a daily massage using your thumb to rub either hand or nail cream into the nail bed. Or make your own moisturizer with 1 teaspoon of olive oil and 1 teaspoon of vitamin E oil—this is a good nighttime nourisher. And practice this hand exercise: Bend the fingers of both hands in toward your palms so the nails of both hands are touching. Then gently rub the nails against each other for one minute to stimulate blood flow.

Buff

10 Nail Enemies:

- *metal nail file*
- *cuticle clippers (except to snip hangnails)*
- *harsh polish remover*
- *nail scissors (save them for your toes)*
- *dark polish (with no base coat)*
- *permanent false nails*

11 **A French manicure is only for those with shortish nails.** Try one on long nails and you'll look every inch the '60s siren. Buy a French manicure kit or make up your own with a bottle of light pink polish and a bottle of white. Cover your nails with a coat of pink; next, line the tips with white (you need a steady hand for this but practice helps); then apply another coat of pink polish over all. For a more subtle effect, use a cream polish instead of white and you won't have to worry about being so careful with the brush either.

12 **Faking fantastic nails has never been easier.** To hide nasty nails, buy acrylic kits that come with their own adhesive and can be cut to fit. Fussy, but cheap. For a professional result, go to a salon that can attach acrylic tips that go halfway up your nail. But beware permanent falsies. Keeping your nails under cover for too long will lead to splitting, staining, and even infections, so never wear false nails for longer than two weeks at one time, and give your nails a two-week holiday in between.

13 **If you treasure your long nails,** never plunge your hands into a bag without looking first. And practice opening and closing zippers with the sides of your fingers.

14 **Not so long ago, the most popular shades of nail polish were ones that matched your lipstick** (think pink, peach, red, and plum). But nail decoration has become more and more elaborate, and thanks to its appearance on the fashion runways, it is now the new jewelry (far cheaper than a diamond ring). Nail-art kits are available for home use, or treat yourself and visit a salon for something really special.

15 **Nail polish takes a whole eight hours to dry rock hard.** Apply polish an hour before bedtime to give your nails a rest while they dry, or hold your hands under cold running water to harden polish in double-quick time. Other speedy techniques include smoothing baby oil over just-dried color or investing in a quick-dry spray. But don't bother waving your hands in the air. This will just make your manicure uneven.

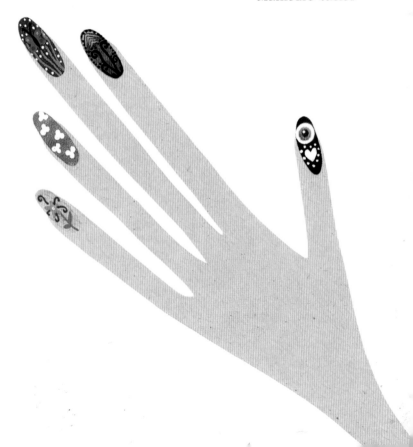

16 **Stained nails? Scrub them with a nailbrush and warm soapy water every day until they shine.** For more serious staining, a soaking in denture cleaner will do the job. Or mix together the juice of 1 lemon with 2 teaspoons of olive oil. Dangle your hands in it for 15 minutes and while the lemon's bleaching, the oil will be nourishing. Medical note: Any green or yellow discolorations at the base of your nails should be looked at by your doctor since this could be a sign of infection.

17 **Weak and wimpy nails?** Wear a coat of clear polish to protect them (but remember to give your nails a rest from polish for one day in six). When filing, leave your old polish on so your nails are stronger and less likely to split. Both cider vinegar and lemon juice are natural nail strengtheners. Drink a glass of water containing 1 tablespoon of either, or if you can't stomach swallowing it, soak your nails in the mixture instead.

18 **Ridges that run up your nail can be caused by damage to the nail bed** (too much prodding and pushing back of those cuticles), a yeast infection, or a zinc deficiency. Regular buffing can smooth them out, and invest in a ridge-filling base coat to use under polish for a pristine paint job.

19 Chipped polish is not a classy look.

Make your manicure last as long as possible by applying a fresh layer of color every night. Do this just before you go to bed and then lie with your hands outside the covers so the shade can dry dent-free. Or for quick and easy touch-ups, invest in a polish pen, which is a no-spill alternative to the traditional bottled polish. To use, shake the pen well and then press down on a piece of paper to get the color flowing before applying to your nails.

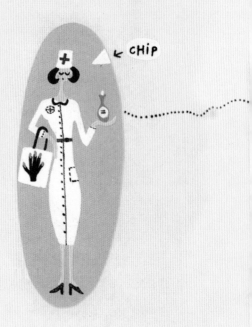

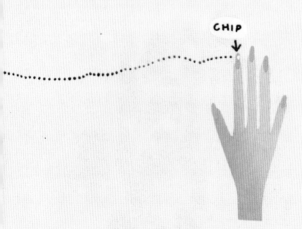

CHIP

20 **Nail hardeners reduce the amount of moisture in your nails** so they're less likely to bend and break. But leave hardener on for only a week or you could dry out your nails too much. The result? Brittle nails that break for a completely different reason.

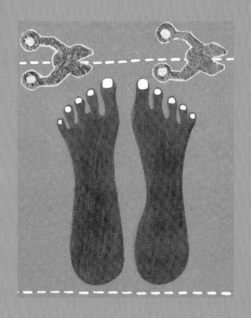

chapter 2

Perfect pedicure

21 Stuck with a bottle of harsh polish remover? Don't throw it away. Add a teaspoon of glycerine (available at drugstores) to the bottle of acetone and it won't be nearly so drying on your nails.

22 Before applying polish, remove any residue of oil or hand lotion or your shade won't stick. Rinse your nails in warm soapy water or wipe with a little nail varnish remover.

23 Always use cotton balls or pads to remove nail varnish. Tissue won't hold the remover or absorb the color, and you'll end up with sticky polish all over your hands as well as your toes.

24 Double-duty treat for feet:

1. To strengthen nails, first soak your feet in warm water with a tablespoon of baking soda added to the mix.

2. Next, cut open a capsule of vitamin E and rub the oil into your nails and cuticles. This is the cheapest, richest moisturizer you can buy, and it will nourish your nails and help prevent splitting.

25 To make your own soaking solution, add any of these to a bowl of warm water and relax for 15 minutes of bliss for your feet:

- *Epsom salts, to relieve sore muscles.*
- *Dead Sea salts, to revive tired and swollen feet.*
- *A few drops of almond oil, to soften the skin.*
- *A few drops of peppermint oil, to revive and refresh.*
- *A few drops of tea tree oil, to help fight fungal infections and odor.*
- *A few drops of lavender oil, to heal and ease fatigue.*
- *3 teaspoons of mustard mixed with water, to warm cold feet.*

- *If you're brave, finish with a plunge in cold water for the quickest pick-me-up in history.*

26 If you're on vacation, go for long walks on the beach: The sand will exfoliate your feet naturally and leave them feeling smoother than any pumice stone. Oh, and it'll make your nails gleam, too. Or if you're stuck at home, a handful of coarse sea salt will do the same thing (without the view). To remind you of that beach, bring a bit of sand back home with you and add a dribble of any vegetable oil. Mix into a paste and massage onto your feet, concentrating on the rough areas.

27 **No. 1 toenail rule: Always cut them straight across.** Heard the one about ingrown toenails being caused by rounding down the sides? Well, it's true. (The other main cause of ingrown toenails is pantyhose that is too small.) Use nail scissors to cut your toenails square and then switch to the coarse side of an emery board to smooth down any sharp edges. If your toenails are very hard, do this after a bath or shower, when the warm water has softened them. And avoid clippers since these can easily split nails as they snip.

28 **Don't go near your nails with anything sharp.** For pushing back cuticles or cleaning under nails, use an orange stick with the top wrapped in cotton. Make sure it is well-padded and you won't do any harm.

29 **When pushing back your cuticles, don't look for that little moon shape at the base of each nail.** Cuticles protect the growing part of your nail, so you don't want to get rid of them entirely. And remember, everybody has different size "moons" so don't try comparing them!

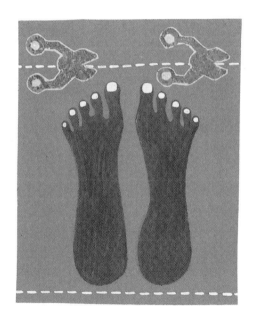

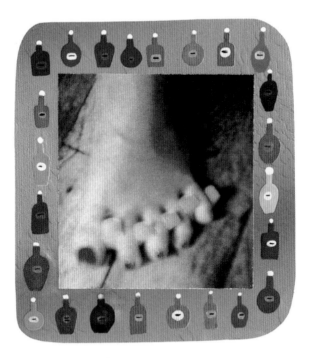

30 **Use toe spacers to make applying polish easier,** or place cotton balls between your toes to keep them from touching each other and smudging your work.

31 **Treat your feet to a regular moisture boost.** Smooth on a body lotion or make your own foot balm with 1 tablespoon of malt vinegar and a 5-oz container of plain yogurt. Leave the mixture on for five minutes before rinsing.

32 **The best time to tackle rough, dry skin is in the bath.** Let the warm water soften your skin for about 10 minutes and then go to work with a pumice stone (synthetic ones are best for real "elephant" skin). Use small, firm, circular movements all around your soles and heels, concentrating on stubborn hard areas. Or invest in a foot file, but don't be too rough with that see-sawing motion.

33 **Most makeup likes the cool inside of your refrigerator come summer,** but nail polish is happy in there any time of the year. In fact, storing polish in the refrigerator will ensure even application with no blobs—and the bottle will last longer.

34 **Instead of shaking your bottle of color madly in the air before application,** copy the professionals and just turn it upside down a few times to mix all the ingredients without churning them up.

35 **The quickest way to turn daytime nails into something a bit more special** is just to add a coat of clear sparkly polish over your old color. It'll help prolong the life of what's underneath, too.

36 **Haven't the time or energy to paint your fingernails?** Then color your toenails instead. They're quicker and easier to do, you don't have to avoid handling anything while the polish dries, and the result will always last much longer than the average manicure, mainly because your toes don't suffer the number of bumps your fingers do.

37 **Any product made for manicures is fine for your pedicures, too.** Your nails are exactly the same on your fingers and toes!

38 **It's easier to be outrageous with colors and patterns on your toenails than your fingernails:** Your fingers are on view all the time, but you can choose where and when your toes are seen—so be adventurous.

39 **Follow these three steps and get a perfect finish:**

Base coat stops dark colored polishes from staining your nails, gives you a smooth surface to paint over, and helps polish stay longer on the nail.

Nail polish comes in hundreds of varieties, from sheer washes (the newest way to color), one-coat wonders (for speedy nails), and long-lasting formulas (available in just about every color you could wish for). Always turn the bottle upside down to mix the polish before applying to ensure your color goes on smoothly.

Top coat is important since it helps protects your polish color from chipping, it prolongs the life of your handiwork, and leaves behind a high shine.

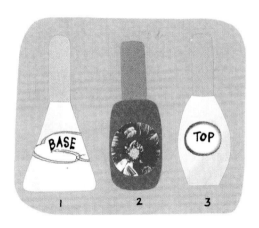

QUICK DRY

40 **Nail polish dries to the touch in a few minutes** but takes many more hours before it's dent-proof. Remember this if you're going for a pedicure; don't pull on socks too soon after or they'll stick to your toes. Ask your pedicurist to use a quick-dry spray, and wear open-toed sandals or flip-flops home. Another idea is to schedule one more beauty appointment afterward. For pedicures at home, hold your toes under cold running water for a few seconds or gently massage in a drop of baby oil (which also moisturizes your cuticles) to speed up the drying process.

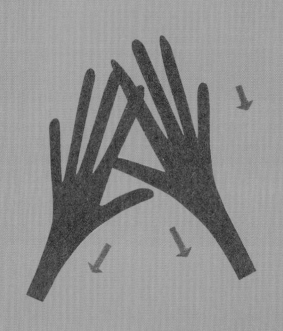

chapter 3

Special care for hands

41 **The everyday nailbrush is a much-ignored beauty buy.** Use it to clean your hands and you'll get an exfoliation treatment, too. And a brush also allows you to get right under your nails to scrub away any grime without damaging the nail bed underneath.

42 **Wash your hands regularly to prevent infections.** Also, it's better to cough and sneeze into the crook of your arm or a tissue than into your hands; rubbing your eyes or shaking hands afterward will spread your germs.

43 **Essential oils can be used to heal and pamper hands in need of help. Choose one that suits your skin type…**

- *Benzoin moisturizes dry, chapped skin and peps up poor circulation.*
- *Camomile soothes inflamed skin.*
- *Eucalyptus heals wounds and insect bites.*
- *Marjoram eases aches and pains and arthritis.*
- *Patchouli treats dermatitis, eczema, and skin sores.*
- *Pine helps reduce excess perspiration.*

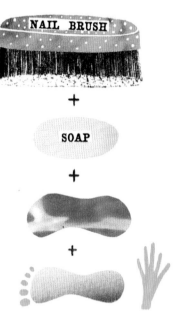

51

44 Save your squeezed lemon halves and use them to deep-clean stained hands. Any discoloration will bleach away to nothing after a good rubbing with lemon juice. As well as brightening up your hands, use lemons to lighten dark elbows. Sit with each one resting inside half a squeezed lemon. This is far kinder than abrasive scrubs and chemical cleaners (and it smells nicer, too).

Special care for hands

45 **The more you moisturize,** the more you're protecting your hands from what they have to go through every day. Keep a pump bottle of hand lotion by every sink in your house and a quick press will soon become second nature. And slather hand lotion on after washing: It will help lock in all that extra moisture. During the winter months, keep your hand lotion near a radiator or register; the warmth helps it sink in faster.

46 **Get into the habit of applying a bit more moisturizer than normal to your face,** and then rub any extra onto the backs of your hands.

47 **You treat your face to a regular mask—why not your hands?** They suffer the same environmental stresses, plus all the hard work you make them do. Mix 1 tablespoon of oatmeal and 1 teaspoon each of olive oil, lemon juice, and glycerine. Add a little water and mix to a stiff paste. Smooth the mixture over your hands. Relax for 20 minutes, or pop on warmed cotton gloves and let the mixture melt into your skin overnight.

48 **Treat your hands to an intensive moisturizing mask** that you can whip up in your kitchen. In a blender, combine a handful of chopped dried apricots (contain vitamin A for healing damaged skin cells) with 1 tablespoon of plain yogurt and 1 tablespoon of honey. Process until smooth, spread generously over your hands and nails, and leave for 20 minutes. Rinse off with warm water.

49 **If your hands are in desperate need of some moisture,** massage in a little warm olive oil (heat it in a saucer over a pan of boiling water). Then put on a pair of warmed cotton gloves. You'll wake up with the softest hands of your life!

50 **The shelves in your local drugstore are bulging with anti-aging creams for your face,** and now you can buy the same for your hands. Look for labels that say "antiwrinkle" or "antiaging," and chances are they'll protect your hands from damaging UV light. Use regularly for about six weeks and your skin will look brighter. Age spots may even start to fade.

51 **Thin skin on the back of your hands can mean that veins show through.** If yours are obvious, use a dab of sunless tanning lotion to darken the skin and hide the veins underneath.

52 Wear rubber gloves for every household task, especially if your hands are in water. (Most models won't even wash their hair without putting a pair on first.) Or before washing the dishes, smooth olive oil over your hands, then put petroleum jelly on top. Pull on a pair of disposable plastic gloves (you won't want to use them again), then your rubber ones. While your hands are in hot water, the oil will be sinking deep into your skin.

53 Your hands show your age sooner than almost any other part of your body. (You'll never see a picture of an aging starlet resting her chin on her hands!) Hands have thinner skin, less fat, and fewer oil glands than your face, and they get treated worse. Daily dunkings in water and chemical cleaners strip the natural oils from your skin, and your hands are out there in all weather. Sun exposure is the reason for age spots and prematurely wrinkled skin, so to protect your hands during the summer, keep a bottle of sunscreen by the sink or front door and apply before going outside. Or choose a hand lotion with an SPF15 and use all year round. But beware very high SPF factors if you're wearing nail polish since they can turn your color yellow.

54 When moisturizing your hands, take a minute longer to give yourself a mini-massage. Work in small circular motions over your joints and then gently pull each finger to ease the joints (but stop short of cracking your knuckles!). Turn your hands over and massage the palms, working up toward the wrists. Lastly, massage the point where your thumb and forefinger are joined; this is an acupressure point that releases a flow of energy to your face.

55 Stress knots don't just happen in your shoulders. Massage each hand and, while you're at it, search out those small stress lumps. You'll be giving your muscles a relaxing kneading and relieving stress at the same time.

56 **Anyone working on a keyboard is at risk for carpal tunnel syndrome,** also known as repetitive stress injury. This is caused by constant repetitive movements and the best way to protect yourself is with hand exercises. It's also a good idea to invest in a wrist support to use while typing, and try not to type for long periods without taking a break.

1. Shake your hands out until they feel completely relaxed and limp.

2. Clench your fingers into a ball and then slowly release and stretch them out.

3. Circle them from the wrist as deeply as possible four times in each direction.

57 **Take up the piano.** Experts agree that piano playing promotes strength and suppleness, which means in later years you'll still have flexible fingers!

66

58 **Don't even think about weeding the garden without first slipping on a pair of protective gloves.** Apart from coming between you and something slippery and/or slimy, gloves will protect against grazing, cuts, and broken nails.

59 **Hands need regular scrubs to get rid of hard skin.** Rough spots aren't just unattractive; they can also crack and let in bacteria. Mix up a handful of sea salt and a tablespoon of glycerine for a cheap homemade exfoliant.

60 **Protect your hands against painful cracked skin and chilblains** by wearing gloves everyday in the winter. Even if the sun is shining, a cold wind can do untold damage to your extremities!

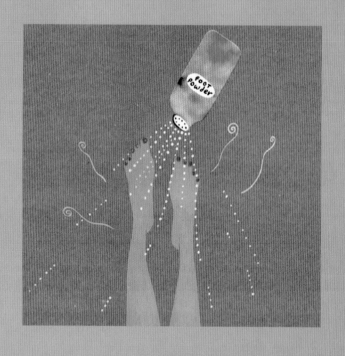

chapter 4

Special care for feet

61 **A quick way to revive tired feet** is to give them a hydrotherapy treatment. Dunk them first in cold water for about 30 seconds and then in warm water for about three minutes. You will get your circulation pumping, which has been known to help prevent varicose veins. Finish by wrapping both feet in a towel and lying down for 20 minutes with your legs slightly elevated.

COLD   HOT

62 **When a long day on your feet leaves you with swollen ankles,** lie on the floor with your feet resting against the wall at a 45-degree angle to your body. Relax for 10 minutes, and then get your circulation going with a foot massage. To avoid swollen ankles on a plane, drink water instead of tea, coffee, or alcohol.

63 **Turn a foot soak into a healing experience** by adding up to six drops of an essential oil. Here's what a few can do:

- *Myrrh treats chilblains and athlete's foot and encourages good circulation.*
- *Rosemary treats rheumatism and stimulates circulation.*
- *Tea tree oil helps heal athlete's foot and warts.*
- *Vetiver eases stiff joints and muscles and soothes aches and pains.*
- *Lemon treats warts and improves circulation.*
- *Black pepper warms sore muscles.*

64 **For an easy foot workout,** invest in a foot massage roller and place it on the floor in front of your couch. Use it to stimulate all those pressure points that have suffered too much stress during the day. Alternatively, fill a bowl with warm water and drop some marbles into the bottom. Now pop your feet in and roll them around it. Blissful.

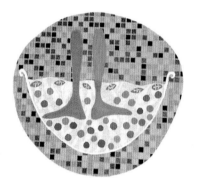

65 **The skin on your feet is the least lubricated on your whole body.** Keep your feet soft and smooth by remembering to include them when you apply body lotion after a bath. Or make a moisturizing foot bath with a handful of powdered milk in a bowl of warm water, and soak your feet for 15 minutes. But steer clear of this if you suffer from sweaty feet—extra cream will just make them more clammy. For extra-dry or cracked feet, try this intensive overnight treatment: Warm some olive oil, then mas-sage into your feet, concentrating on the rough areas. Then slip on a pair of cotton socks, and slide into bed.

66 **During your lifetime, you'll walk the equivalent of four times around the earth.** When your feet feel like they've done a lifetime's exercise in one day, rub those tired, aching soles with either cider vinegar or lemon juice to revive them. Or make your own pick-me-up rub with a few drops of stimulating peppermint oil mixed with any vegetable oil.

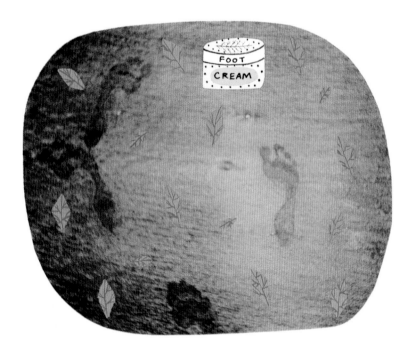

67 The best part of a professional pedicure? The foot massage. This will invigorate your whole body plus relax your mind, and it's worth watching carefully to repeat at home when you're on your last legs. And the good thing about it is you don't need to be an expert. Feet have 72,000 nerve endings so you're bound to hit the spot occasionally!

1. Smooth any massage oil over your feet.

2. Knead the soles of both feet with your thumbs. Lean into your hands and rotate in small circles all over the undersides.

3. Now use your thumbs on the tops of your feet and slide down towards your toes, working between the tendons.

4. Finish by extending the massage around your ankles, working in larger circles, and up your calves with long strokes, always moving in the direction of your heart.

68 If you have difficulty getting off to sleep, try rubbing the soles of your feet with sesame seed oil (which also works as an anti-inflammatory) just before going to bed. Use your thumbs to knead the underside and feel your body slowly relax.

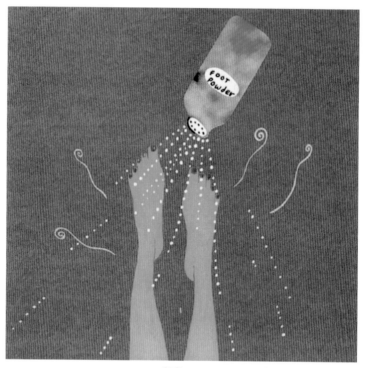

78

69 **A sprinkling of talcum powder in your shoes during the hot summer months will help keep them dry and slip free.** But a better idea is to invest in a specially formulated foot powder that absorbs sweat, combats odor, and helps prevent damp problems (think athlete's foot) without caking into lumps of white mush like some starch-based powders.

70 **Feet don't stay the same size once you've grown up.** Get your feet measured professionally once a year or check them yourself at home. Stand barefoot on a piece of paper. Make a mark behind your heel and in front of your longest toe. Cut a strip between the two points. Slip it inside your shoe. There should be between $\frac{1}{2}$ and 1 inch between the end of the paper and the heel of your shoe.

71 **Stop smoking and your feet will feel warmer.** A podiatrist can tell instantly if a client smokes, because smokers tend to have dry, cold feet that show they have been starved of oxygen.

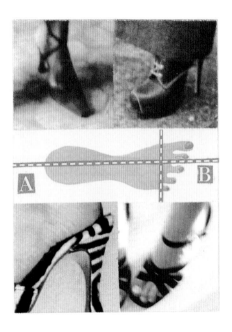

72 **Vary the height of your heels and you'll save yourself from backache,** poor posture, and sore muscles. And high-heel addicts be warned: In time, you may actually develop shorter calf muscles—which means you won't be able to put your heels flat on the ground!

73 **Go late-night shoe shopping rather than running out at lunchtime.** Your feet will be more swollen later in the day, so there'll be less chance of your buying shoes that are too small and that will pinch you forever more.

74 **Hard, calloused heels look nasty in strappy sandals** and are murder on socks and panty hose. Save on your hosiery budget by coming to grips with your rough skin after a 10-minute soak in the bathtub. Use a pumice stone and work in small, circular movements. But be careful if you've soaked for too long and your skin's gotten spongy—it's easy to whisk away way too much. And save your panty hose toes by trimming toenails regularly once a week, followed by a quick smoothing with the coarse side of an emery board.

75 The average foot pumps out half a pint of perspiration a day (that's enough to fill two egg cups), so it's not surprising your feet can smell by the day's end. In the winter, replace synthetic socks with cotton ones and slip cotton inner soles into your shoes. Soaking your feet in a footbath with 6 drops of cypress oil added to the water will also fight any lingering smell. Alternatively sprinkle a tablespoon of sea salt into the water. This will help correct the pH balance of your skin and neutralize any nasty odors.

76 With around 120,000 sweat glands, the natural smell of your feet is said to be a sexual stimulant. If you're not convinced and want guaranteed odor-free feet, wipe the soles with rubbing alcohol in the morning and at night, and you'll be able to fling off your shoes with confidence.

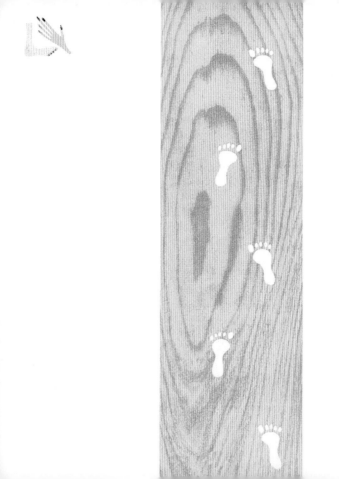

77 Get into the habit of going bare foot at home to keep your feet toned (much more comfy on carpet than on trendy bare floors).

78 Every time your feet take a step, they have to absorb twice your body weight. So never miss an opportunity to put your feet up and give them a rest. And be kind to your feet by using cushioned innersoles in your shoes to ease the strain.

79 **Can't see where you're walking when your feet are underwater?** Then pop on a pair of jelly sandals and you'll protect your feet from all sorts of scary things, including coral scratches, biting fish, and any other slimy creature you could step on by mistake!

80 **Feet respond to exercise, too.** In winter, wiggle bare toes to boost circulation and prevent chilblains. Simply revolving ankles first one way and then the other will help keep joints supple and soothe swollen ankles. All that walking given you a charley horse? Lie on the floor with your feet resting against the wall and spread your toes wide as you slowly "walk up" it.

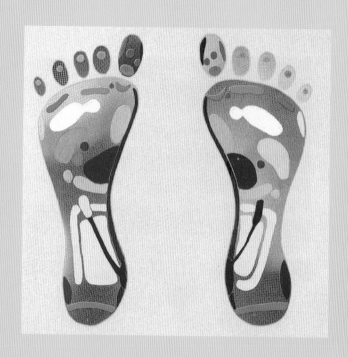

chapter 5

Treatments and therapies

81 **Athlete's foot is a fungus infection easily picked up where other bare feet have been.** It grows best in warm, moist areas, such as between your toes, and looks white because the outer layer of skin is wet. Attack athlete's foot with regular applications of tea tree oil between your toes. Dab onto feet using a damp cotton ball, concentrating on the affected areas. Or try cotton balls soaked in vinegar or lemon juice. For inflamed blistering, make a weak salt solution with 1 level teaspoon of ordinary table salt added to 1 pint of lukewarm water. You've heard it before, but remember to dry between your toes and wear flip-flops when walking around fungus breeding grounds like swimming pool locker rooms. Other fungus fighters include keeping your feet dry and changing your socks (cotton or wool are best) every day. Also, alternate shoes so they have a chance to dry out on their day off. And kick them off as soon as you get home.

82 **Sweaty, smelly feet are more common than you think,** so don't be embarrassed if your own start to stink. Suddenly sweaty feet can be a sign of nervousness (and the same goes for sweaty palms), so when you're stressed, use a special antiperspirant spray for your feet or an

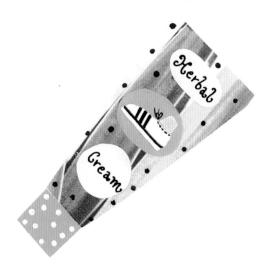

odor-control spray for your shoes. What you wear will also help. Lightweight shoes with leather soles are your best bet; synthetic materials and thick rubber soles won't let your feet breathe.

83 **A plantar wart loves warm, sweaty places.** These small lumps of dead skin cells protrude just above the surface and look a bit like a mini-cauliflower. They're caused by a virus and it takes your body about two years to build up a resistance, at which time your wart may disappear overnight. If your wart is painful and you can't wait that long, an over-the-counter solution may work. But as these warts are usually very deep, you may need to see a dermatologist or podiatrist, who can freeze the area and then burn off the hard skin (you won't feel a thing). And while you're infected, do everyone else a favor and cover your wart with a waterproof bandage if you plan to walk barefoot in public places.

84 **Chilblains are thought to be caused by bad circulation and cold weather,** but why only some people get them is a bit of a mystery. If you're one of the unlucky few, keep your hands and feet warm, don't wear tight-fitting gloves or shoes—they will constrict circulation—and avoid sudden temperature changes. Warm up gradually when you come in from the cold (no rushing straight to the fire).

85 **Everyone gets cold hands and feet in the winter,** but if your fingers or toes turn white or blue and then red as they warm up again, chances are you're suffering from the very common Raynaud's syndrome. This circulation disorder is nine times more common in women than men, and those in their teens and 20s are even more susceptible. Raynaud's is the constriction of the small blood vessels in your fingers and toes when exposed to cold or a change in temperature. To stop a painful attack, wear lots of layers in the winter (cotton gloves under wool ones, ditto with socks). Smoking further constricts the blood vessels. You could also try taking a circulation-boosting supplement such as ginger, ginkgo biloba, vitamin E, or evening primrose oil.

86 **Most foot problems are caused by rubbing and pressure from badly fitted shoes.** Change your shoes and the pain should stop. A podiatrist is the person to see with bad foot problems, but here's what you can do yourself:

Corns are a thickening of the outer layer of skin that develops a hard central plug—the painful part when pressed. Corns are most common on the small toe where it rubs your shoe. Buy a corn pad to relieve the pressure, and a corn plaster to remove the corn. Wear

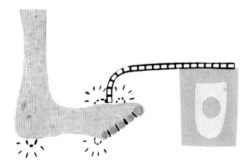

better-fitting shoes or try inserting innersoles in your old ones.

Calluses are caused by too much pressure. These areas of thickened skin often start life as a blister. They're your foot's way of protecting the soft skin underneath. Danger areas are the soles and around prominent bones. Change your shoe style and soak your feet before thinning the skin by rubbing with a pumice product.

Bunions are painful inflammations between your skin and a bone and usually happen at the base of the big toe where it rubs your shoe. Stop wearing the offending shoe, or try an innersole. If your bunion doesn't budge, visit a professional.

87 Your feet will swell up on a plane, so plan ahead and wear loose-fitting shoes. Take them off once you're settled, put on a pair of socks, and then take a trip down the aisle regularly, wiggling and stretching your toes as you go. That way, when you arrive at your destination, you'll be able to fit back into your shoes without having to hobble off the plane (not stylish).

88 How you stand on your feet is all important to your posture, and bad posture can cause all sorts of problems, including back pain, digestive and circulation problems, and headaches. Check your stance by standing facing a full-length mirror with your legs slightly apart. Chances are you're probably standing with all your weight on one leg and your hips twisted to one side. Now stand with your weight evenly distributed and your hips and shoulders level. It might take a little practice, but persevere. Improved posture can reduce stress and insomnia—not to mention tucking in your tummy and adding as much as an inch to your height.

89 **Experts recommend you visit a podiatrist every three months for a foot check.** They can remove any tough skin build up and tackle problems such as corns by trimming away the hardened outer layers of skin and prescribing more potent products than you can buy at the drugstore.

90 **Most of us ignore our feet and then wonder why we suffer with foot problems.** The most important thing to remember is to always wear properly fitting shoes, but research shows that most children wear a size too small (no surprise then that many have bad feet by the time they're teenagers). Ill-fitting shoes cause most foot problems—including deformities of the big toes, bunions, hammer toes, corns, calluses, and ingrown toenails—so make sure your new ones are comfy before buying. And avoid putting on shoes right after washing your feet since athlete's foot loves damp skin in a warm shoe!

91 **Do your own reflexology in the bathtub.** Lie with your feet up against the far end of the tub with a tennis ball under each one. Now, move your feet so the ball moves around under each sole, hitting all those sensitive nerve endings as it rolls.

92 **Reflexology is a popular alternative treatment** based on the idea that your body is divided into 10 zones of energy that can be manipulated to alleviate physical and mental problems. The reflexologist will massage specific points in your feet that correspond with organs in your body. For instance, the ball of each toe is linked to your head, brain, and sinuses, and a strip across your heels correspond to your sciatic nerve. When these points are manipulated, they stimulate the organs, clearing any energy blockages and encouraging them to function better. If you have a problem, it's likely the first few treatments will be uncomfortable because the reflexologist works hardest on your stressed parts. But soon you'll find the treatment completely relaxing and you may even fall asleep.

93 **Learn what parts of your feet correspond with other areas of your body,** and massage your health problems away:

- *Breathing complaints—the fleshy ball of your foot.*
- *Stomach and digestive problems —under the instep.*
- *Backache—the instep between toe and heel.*
- *Eye, ear, nose, and throat ailments —the toes.*
- *Headache—the big toe.*

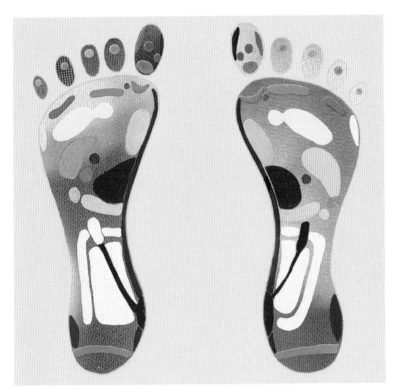

94 Clairvoyants and mystics use hands to work out your characteristics and map out your destiny. The lines on your palms, as well as the shape of your hands and fingers, have long been believed to hold secrets about your past—and future. See the picture opposite for a rough guide to what different lines represent:

- *White—line of life (general health and vitality).*
- *Black—line of fate (how chance affects your life).*

- *Turquoise (running downward)— line of the sun (represents potential for success and happiness).*
- *Pale blue (running across palm)— line of the head (represents capacity for intelligence and memory).*
- *Pink—line of the heart (represents the emotions and the physical health of your heart).*
- *Bright turquoise (at the bottom of the little finger)—lines of affection (represent close relationships and family).*
- *Dark blue—line of travel (represents capacity for enjoying travel).*

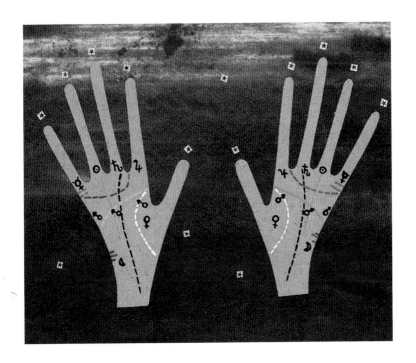

95 **In Buddhism,** the immanence of Buddha is depicted by soles of the feet bearing symbols of divine wisdom. These indicate contact between the earth and divinity. When stressed, stand still and imagine your feet making contact with the floor. Many spiritual healers recommend visualizing roots growing from your feet into the earth for the ultimate grounding experience.

96 **Feeling stressed?** Take a look at how you're sitting. If your legs and arms are tightly crossed, untangle yourself and shake your hands and feet. Then circle them first one way and then the other for an instant calming effect.

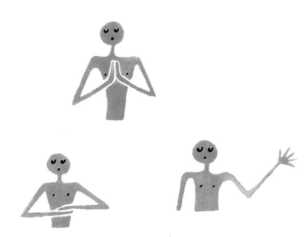

108

97 **Beware—even as you're speaking, your hands may be giving you away.** Clasping hands with another conveys friendship, love, congratulations, and welcome. Even in the business world, a handshake is the mark of good faith. Here's what your hands could be saying about how you're feeling:

- *clenched—threatening*
- *open—giving blessing*
- *raised with fingers open—making a pledge*
- *covered—respectful*
- *folded—tranquil*

98 **"Liver spots" aren't just a problem for your granny.** These dark-pigmented marks found on the backs of hands are caused by sun exposure, not because you're old enough to retire. And they're difficult to get rid of, so protect now or your hands will look old before their time.

99 **Usually associated with Indian brides,** the art of Mehndi is the traditional practice of painting the skin with henna. The plant extract is made into a paste and piped through a bag (a bit like icing a cake) to draw intricate patterns and symbols, most commonly on the feet and hands. A henna tattoo stains the skin with an orange dye that fades gradually over a three-week period. It's thought to bring good luck to the wearer (a new bride won't be expected to do housework until the tattoo wears off!) and to ward off evil spirits. Now, thanks to celebrities and fashion models sporting Mehndi, you can buy kits and create your own designs. But if you don't fancy messing around with smelly henna paste, choose ready-made transfer tattoos instead.

100 **Hands have been used for centuries to heal.** Reiki is an ancient method of healing that involves the practitioner laying their hands on or above your body to direct energy to the areas where it's most needed. Some of the ailments that respond well to Reiki are back pain, headaches, insomnia, depression, anxiety, and low energy.

Illustrator's dedication:
To my family.

Author's dedication:
This book is dedicated to my mother and father.

Published by MQ Publications Limited
12 The Ivories, 6–8 Northampton Street, London, N1 2HY
Tel: 020 7359 2244 / Fax: 020 7359 1616
email: mqpublications.com

Text © Liz Wilde 2000
Illustrations © Carol Morley 2000

Cover design: Broadbase
Interior design: The Big Idea
Series Editor: Elizabeth Carr

ISBN: 1-84072-028-X

3 5 7 9 0 8 6 4 2

Printed in China